Made in the USA
Columbia, SC
12 August 2022

65232285R00063